WONDER WHY Book of

STARS

Written by Patrick Moore
Illustrated by Raymond Turvey

GROSSET & DUNLAP
A FILMWAYS COMPANY
Publishers • New York

THE STARS IN THE SKY

"Twinkle, twinkle little star,
How I wonder what you are . . . ."
Most of you will have heard this old rhyme, but do you know what the stars really are?

When the sky is dark, you can see many stars. All of them look like dots of light. They seem small because they are so far away from us, but they are really very big and hot. Each star is a **sun**, and our own Sun is only a star. The Sun seems so much bigger and brighter than the other stars because it is so much closer to us.

The Earth moves round the Sun, but the stars do not. Many of the stars you can see at night-time are much more powerful than our Sun, though we also know of stars which are much less powerful than the Sun.

stars are
re all the
e, but they
too faint to
seen when
Sun has
n.

We cannot see the stars in the daytime because the sky is too bright.

If the Sun were taken out to the distance of any of the stars, it too would look like a speck of light.

1

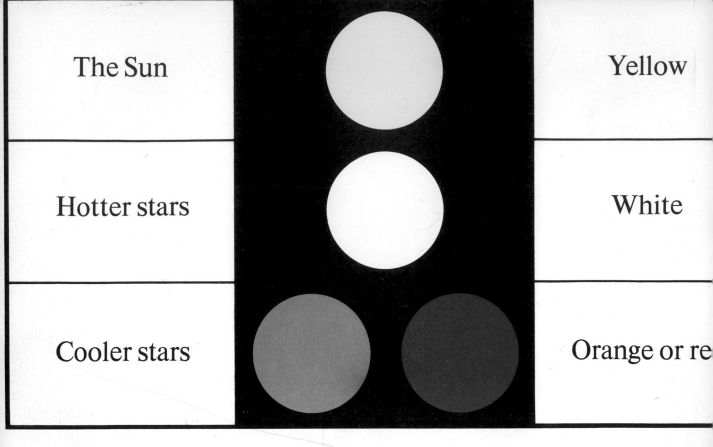

The Sun		Yellow
Hotter stars		White
Cooler stars		Orange or re

White stars are very hot, and most of them are much brighter than the Sun.

The Sun is a **yellow star**.

Yellow stars are of two kinds. Some are very like the Sun, others are much larger and more powerful.

Red and **orange stars** are cooler then yellow stars, and are either very huge and bright or dim and small.

THE SUN IS A STAR

The Sun is a **star**. It is a great ball, made up of gas, and very hot indeed. It sends us all our light and heat, and without it there could be no life on Earth.

The distance between the Sun and the Earth is 150 million kilometres (93 million miles). This is a very long way, but the stars are much more distant still. If you draw a line 2.5 centimetres long, and let this line stand for the distance between the Earth and the Sun, the nearest star will have to be taken over 6.5 kilometres away. No wonder that the stars look so much smaller and fainter than the Sun!

The Sun is the only star which is close enough for us to study really well. When we learn about the Sun, we are also learning about the other stars.

2

KEY
A Corona
B Chromosphere
C Outer Layer
D Middle Layer
E Core

The **Corona** is the outer part of the Sun's atmosphere.

The **Chromosphere** is made of very very hot gases which shoot up at high speed into the Corona.

Heat is sent to the surface of the Sun, through the **Middle** and **Outer** layers, from the **Core**.

The temperature of the **Core** is over 14,000,000°C.

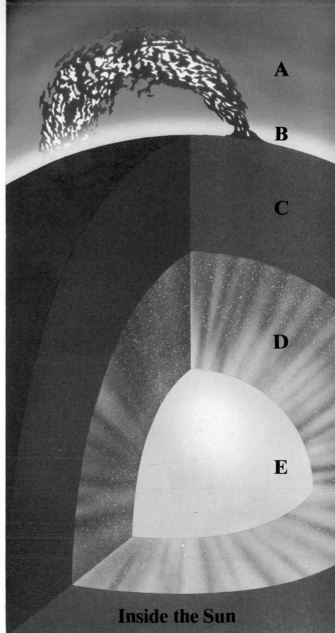

Inside the Sun

Sun

Earth

The **diameter** (width) of the Sun is 109 times that of the Earth.

Light takes 8.3 minutes to reach us from the Sun, so we see the Sun as it was 8.3 minutes ago.

There is one thing you must always remember.

If you have a telescope or a pair of field-glasses, NEVER look at the Sun.

If you do, all the Sun's heat will fall on to your eye, and you will blind yourself.

Make A Simple Model of the Earth

Take a ball of wool and push a stick through it as shown in the picture.

Model of the Earth on its axis

Knitting needle

The Earth's axis passes through the North Pole, the centre of the Earth, and the South Pole, as shown in the illustration.

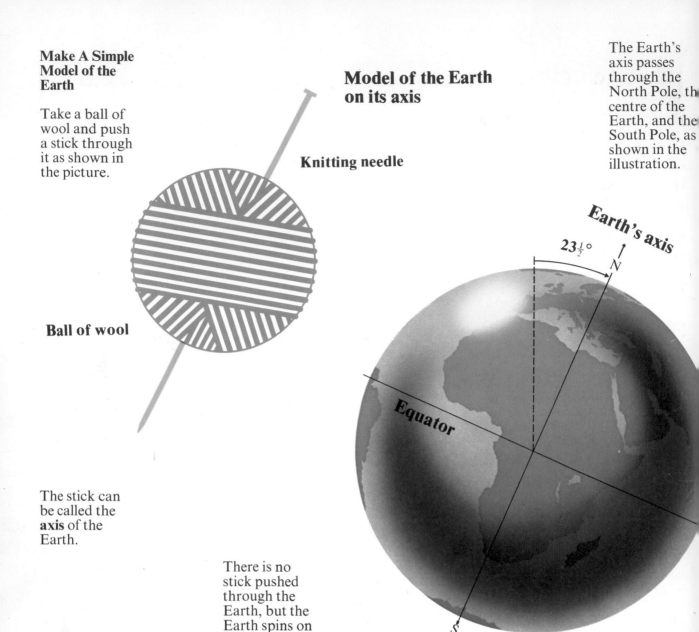

Ball of wool

The stick can be called the **axis** of the Earth.

There is no stick pushed through the Earth, but the Earth spins on its axis.

The Earth's axis is tilted at an angle of $23\frac{1}{2}°$.

People who lived long ago thought that the world must be flat, and they also thought it stayed quite still with the sky moving round it.

Now we know the Earth is round like a big ball, and it is spinning around.

THE EARTH SPINS ROUND THE SUN

The Sun rises in the eastern part of the sky, and sets towards the west. The whole sky seems to be turning round the Earth, taking the Sun, the Moon and the stars with it.

This is not what is really happening. The Earth is shaped like a ball, and it moves round the Sun. As it moves, the Earth spins, making one turn in 24 hours. Because the Earth spins from west to east, the sky seems to turn round from east to west.

It is this spinning of the Earth which makes the sky seem to move.

THE POLE STAR

In the north direction, the axis of the Earth points to a place in the sky close to a star which we call the **Pole Star**. The Pole Star seems to stay almost still, with all the other stars going round it in 24 hours.

From Britain, the Pole star is quite high up. If you could travel to the North Pole of the Earth, you could see the Pole Star straight above your head.

People who live in southern countries, such as Australia, can never see the Pole Star at all. They have a **South Pole Star** of their own, but it is very faint and not easy to recognize.

Pole Star ☆

The **Pole Star** lies due north in the sky.

It is easy to find even though it is not very bright.

The Pole Star is part of a group of stars called the **Little Bear.**

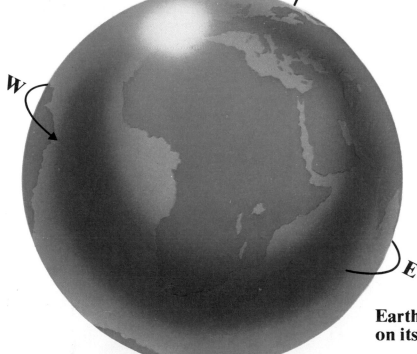

Earth turning on its axis

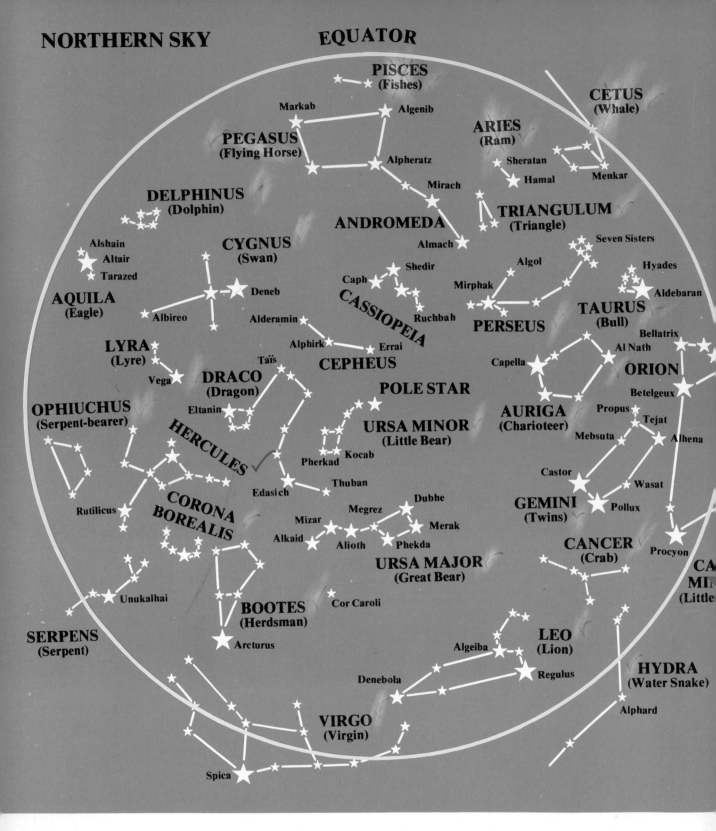

EQUATOR

PISCES
(Fishes)

CETUS
(Whale)

Markab · Algenib

ARIES
(Ram)

PEGASUS
(Flying Horse)

Alpheratz

Sheratan
Hamal
Menkar

Mirach

DELPHINUS
(Dolphin)

TRIANGULUM
(Triangle)

ANDROMEDA

Almach

Seven Sisters

CYGNUS
(Swan)

Shedir
Algol
Hyades

Alshain
Altair
Tarazed

Caph
Mirphak
Aldebaran

Deneb

Ruchbah

CASSIOPEIA

AQUILA
(Eagle)

Albireo

Alderamin

PERSEUS

TAURUS
(Bull)

Bellatrix

LYRA
(Lyre)

Alphirk

Errai

Capella

Al Nath

Vega

Taïs

CEPHEUS

ORION

DRACO
(Dragon)

POLE STAR

AURIGA
(Charioteer)

Betelgeux

OPHIUCHUS
(Serpent-bearer)

Eltanin

URSA MINOR
(Little Bear)

Propus
Tejat

HERCULES

Pherkad Kocab

Mebsuta

Alhena

Edasich

Thuban

Castor

Wasat

Rutilicus

CORONA
BOREALIS

Mizar

Megrez

Dubhe

GEMINI
(Twins)

Pollux

Alkaid

Alioth

Merak

Phekda

CANCER
(Crab)

CA
MI
(Little

Unukalhai

URSA MAJOR
(Great Bear)

Procyon

SERPENS
(Serpent)

BOOTES
(Herdsman)

Cor Caroli

Algeiba

LEO
(Lion)

Arcturus

Regulus

HYDRA
(Water Snake)

Denebola

VIRGO
(Virgin)

Alphard

Spica

The stars which can be seen at any time depend on the season of the year and the place on Earth that you are looking from.

THE CONSTELLATIONS

The stars do not stand still in space. They are moving about very quickly, but they are so far away from us that they seem to keep to the same groups or patterns, which we call **constellations**.

The easiest to learn the constellatio is to seek ou the most ob ones and us them as guid for the othe

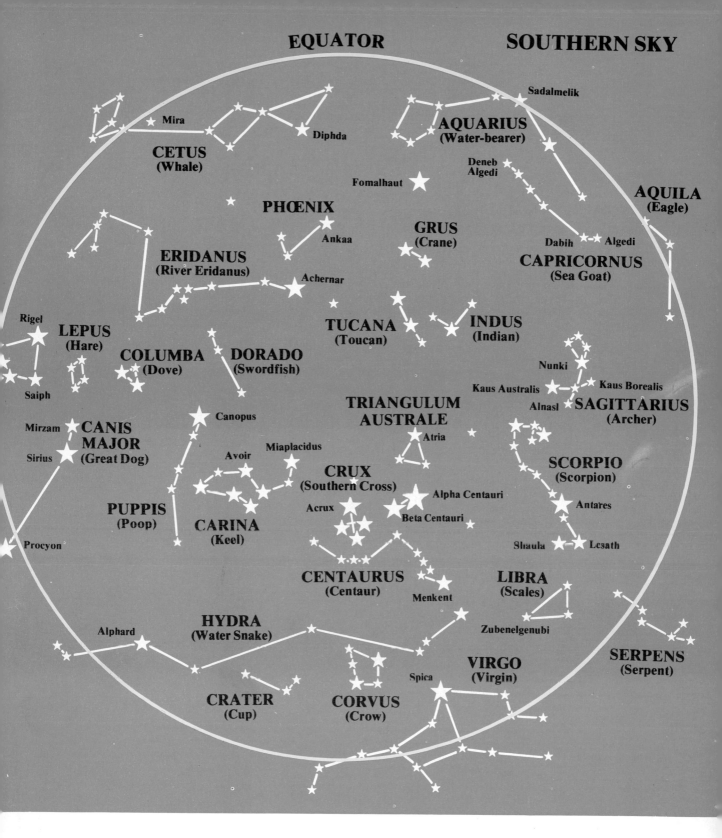

EQUATOR   SOUTHERN SKY

Sadalmelik

Mira

CETUS
(Whale)

Diphda

AQUARIUS
(Water-bearer)

Deneb
Algedi

Fomalhaut

AQUILA
(Eagle)

PHŒNIX

Ankaa

GRUS
(Crane)

Dabih   Algedi

ERIDANUS
(River Eridanus)

Achernar

CAPRICORNUS
(Sea Goat)

Rigel

LEPUS
(Hare)

COLUMBA
(Dove)

DORADO
(Swordfish)

TUCANA
(Toucan)

INDUS
(Indian)

Saiph

Nunki

Kaus Borealis

Mirzam

CANIS
MAJOR
(Great Dog)

Canopus

Avoir   Miaplacidus

TRIANGULUM
AUSTRALE

Kaus Australis

Alnasl

SAGITTARIUS
(Archer)

Atria

Sirius

CRUX
(Southern Cross)

SCORPIO
(Scorpion)

PUPPIS
(Poop)

Acrux

Alpha Centauri

Beta Centauri

Antares

CARINA
(Keel)

Procyon

Shaula   Lesath

CENTAURUS
(Centaur)

Menkent

LIBRA
(Scales)

HYDRA
(Water Snake)

Alphard

Zubenelgenubi

SERPENS
(Serpent)

VIRGO
(Virgin)

Spica

CRATER
(Cup)

CORVUS
(Crow)

---

olden times
ople believed
e sky was solid
d that the
rs were lights
ed onto it.

The Ancient
Chinese, Egyptians
and Greeks were
the first people
to draw maps of
the stars.

They named
star patterns
after people
and animals from
their old stories
and legends.

The constellations
of **Cassiopeia, Orion**
and **Taurus** are
some of these early
patterns.

When explorers
went far south,
they had to
divide much of
the southern
sky into
constellations
for the first
time.

7

THE GREAT BEAR

These constellations have been given names. One of the best known of them is the **Great Bear**, which some people call the **Plough** or the **Big Dipper**.

Because the Great Bear is not far from the Pole Star, it never sets as seen from Britain. It goes round and round the Pole Star, and it can always be seen when the sky is dark and clear. Sometimes it is overhead; at other times you will find it rather low down in the north part of the sky.

There are seven fairly bright stars in the **Great Bear** making up the shape as shown in the picture.

You can see the constellation of the Great Bear in this photograph.

The Great Bear is very easy to pick out in the sky.

Alioth, Alkaid and **Dubhe** are the brightest stars in the Great Bear.

Mizar has a very faint star close beside it known as **Alcor**.

The stars are not all the same distance from us, and so the stars in a constellation are not really close to each other. In the Great Bear, the two stars in the **tail** are called **Alkaid** and **Mizar**. Alkaid is a little the brighter of the two, but it is over twice as far away from us as Mizar.

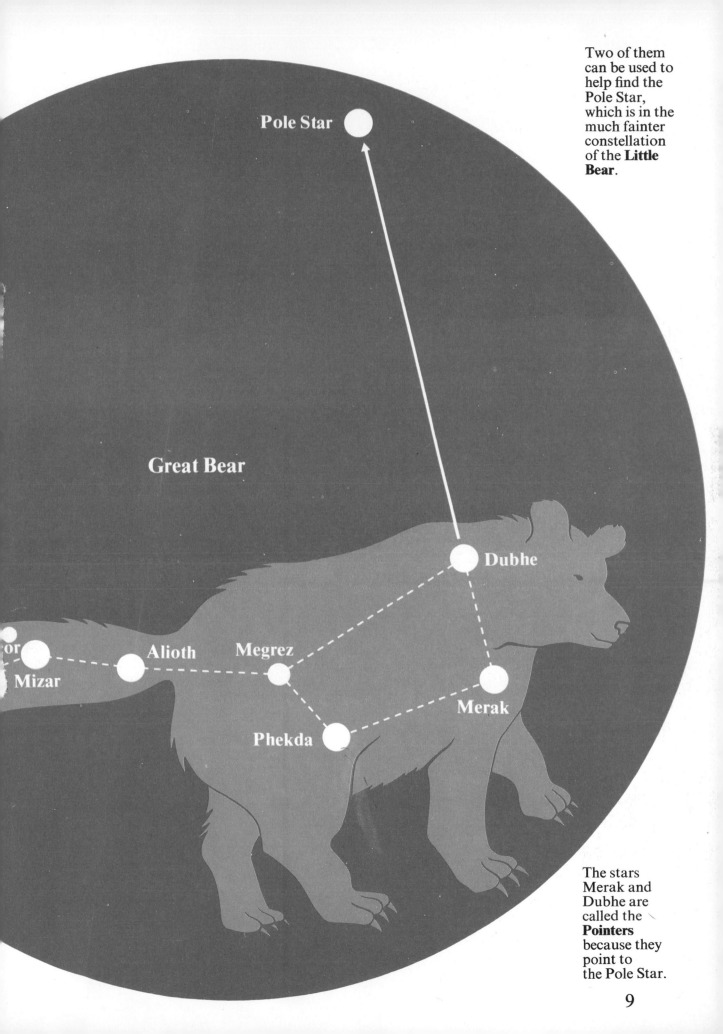

Two of them can be used to help find the Pole Star, which is in the much fainter constellation of the **Little Bear**.

Pole Star

Great Bear

Dubhe

or

Mizar

Alioth

Megrez

Merak

Phekda

The stars Merak and Dubhe are called the **Pointers** because they point to the Pole Star.

9

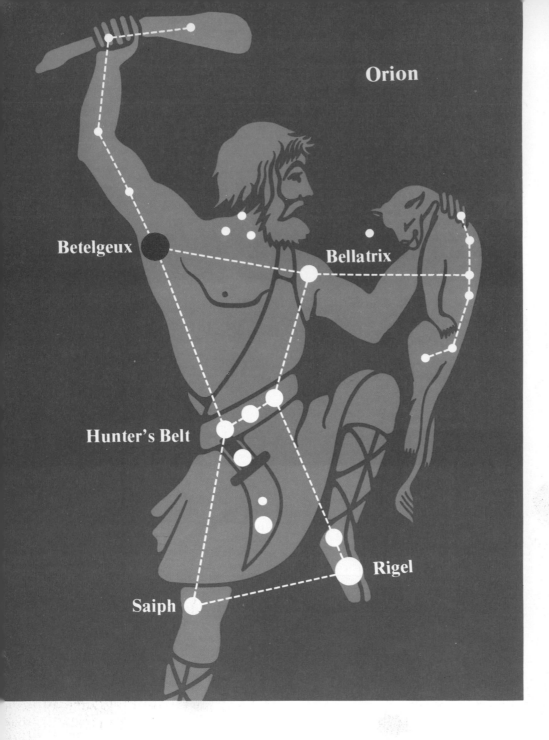

Orion

In the old
stories which
come from
Ancient
Greece, Orion
was a famous
hunter.

Orion said that
he could shoot
and kill any
animal on
Earth, but he
had forgotten
the scorpion,
which stung
him in the heel
and killed him.

The three stars
in the middle
of the
constellations
make up the
Hunter's belt.

The brightest
stars in the
constellation
are **Betelgeux**
which marks
and **Rigel** which
marks one of
his feet.

ORION

Another constellation is **Orion**, which is brighter than
the Great Bear, but is not always visible. During
evenings in winter it is high up in the south as seen
from Britain, but during the middle of the summer it
is so close to the Sun in the sky that we cannot see it at
all.

Orion has two very bright stars, one in the top left of the constellation and the other in the lower right. These two stars have special names: they are called **Betelgeux** and **Rigel**. Betelgeux is a red star, while Rigel is white. All the brightest stars in Orion are thousands of times more powerful than the Sun.

he **Scorpion** is lso in the sky, ut it is in the pposite side f the sky to rion, so that ou can never ee them at the ame time.

It is said that this was done to stop the scorpion from stinging Orion again!

The Scorpion's heart is marked by the very red star Antares.

From Britain, the Scorpion can be seen low in the south during evenings in early summer.

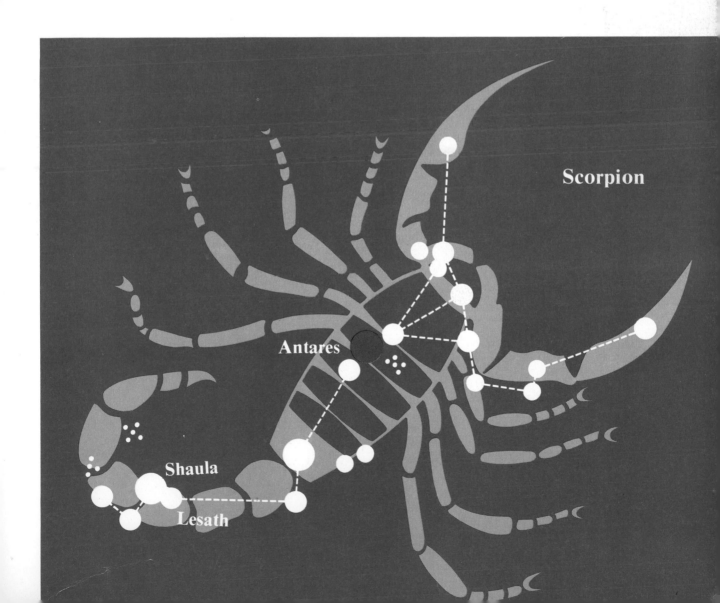

The **Southern Cross** has four bright stars close together in the sky.

It is the smallest of all the constellations.

Not far from it, there are two even more brilliant stars, which point to the Southern Cross, as shown in the picture.

Alpha Centauri is the most brilliant of the two stars pointing to the Southern Cross.

This star is the closest to us of all the bright stars. It is only a little more than four light years away.

Even this is about 400 thousand kilometres!

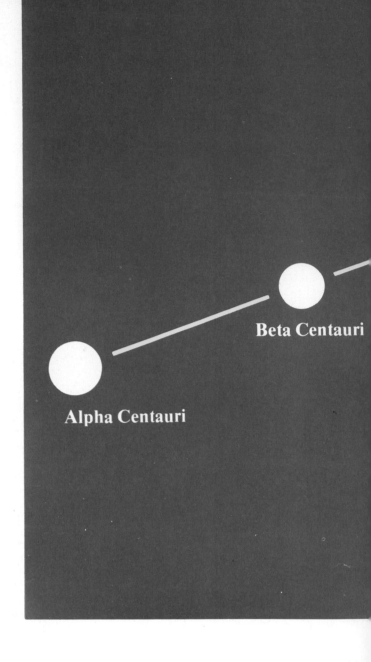

Beta Centauri

Alpha Centauri

THE SOUTHERN CROSS

If you are in Australia, South Africa or New Zealand, you will be able to see some constellations which are not visible from Britain, because they never rise.

One of these is the **Southern Cross**, which is not really shaped like a cross, but is more like a kite.

The Southern Cross is a very small group, much smaller than the Great Bear or Orion, but because its stars are so bright and so close together, it is just as easy to find.

Gamma Crucis is a red star. Its colour makes a sharp contrast to the whiteness of **Acrux** and **Beta Crucis**.

You can see the Southern Cross in this photograph.

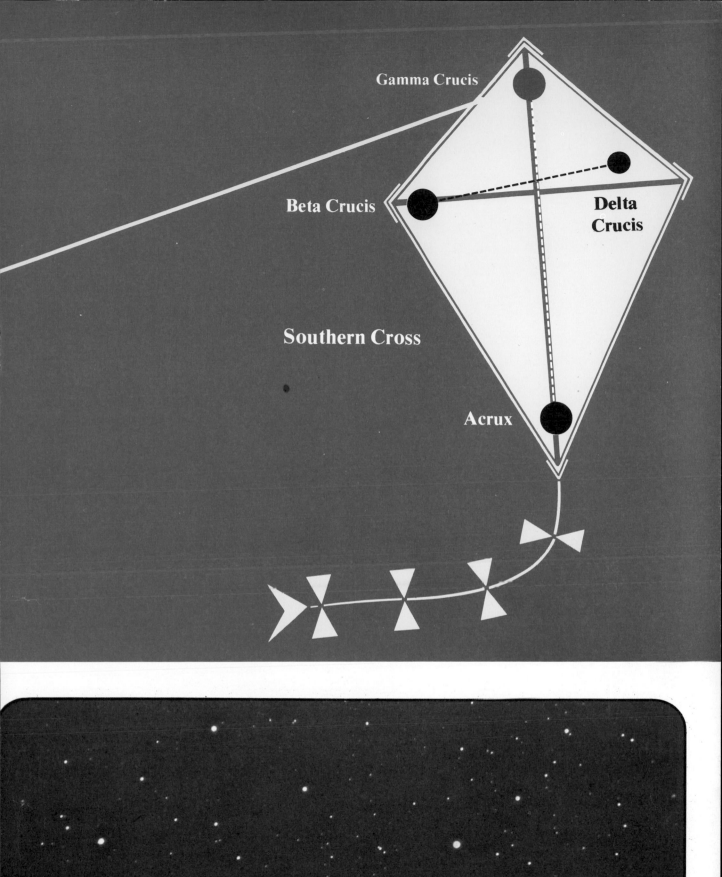

Gamma Crucis

Beta Crucis

Delta
Crucis

Southern Cross

Acrux

If we could land on a far off planet, the stars would be
in different patterns to those we see from Earth.

THE DISTANCE OF THE STARS

The stars are much further away from us than the Sun or the Moon. Even the nearest of the brightest stars is at a distance of over 12,500,000 million kilometres (20 million million miles). Even rays of light, which travel more quickly than anything else we know, take years to come to us from the stars.

The brightest star in the sky is **Sirius** but its light takes $8\frac{1}{2}$ years to reach us. You can see it during winter evenings from Britain below Orion, in line with the three stars of the Hunter's Belt. It seems to twinkle very strongly, because it is always rather low down.

year,
y of light
els almost
illion million
metres (6
ion million
s). This
ance is called
light year.

light from
us takes
ears to
h us. So we
Sirius as
ed to be
ears ago.

Most of the other stars are much further away than Sirius.

Light from **Rigel** the white star in Orion takes 900 years to reach us.

This is why Rigel looks less brilliant in the sky than Sirius, though it is really much more powerful.

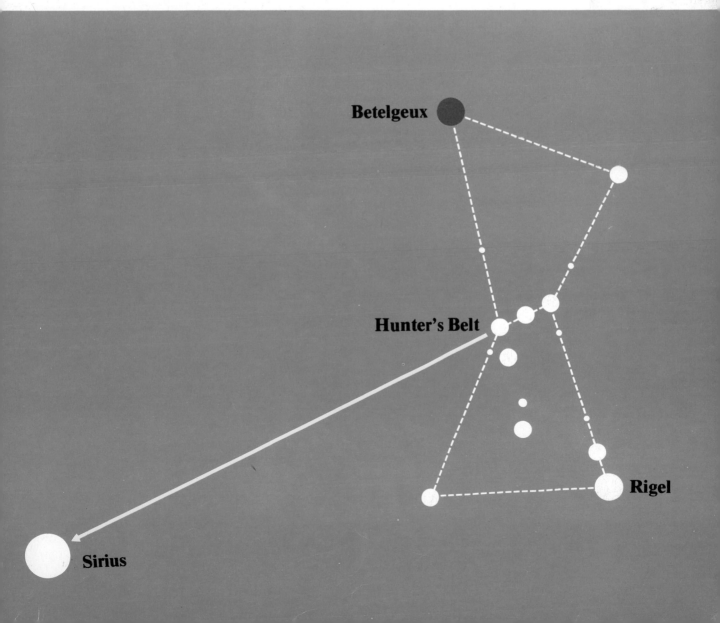

Though the red stars are not as hot as the Sun, some of them are much bigger.

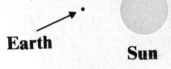

Earth

Sun

Betelgeux

A star which is low in the sky twinkles more than a star which is high up.

This is because its light is travelling through more of the Earth's air.

HEAT AND LIGHT OF THE STARS

If you look at a bright star, you will notice that it is twinkling. This twinkling has nothing to do with the star itself. The light from the star is coming to us through the Earth's air, and is **shaken about**, so that the star seems to twinkle strongly.

Some star colours ca be seen wi the eye bu if you can look at th through a telescope will see th colours m clearly.

Betelgeux and Antares are both so big that if you compare them in size with a football, the Sun will be only the size of a small bead, while the Earth will be no bigger than a grain of sand.

Betelgeux is as powerful as three thousand Suns.

Betelgeux is large enough to swallow the whole path of our Earth round the Sun.

The stars are not all alike. The Sun, as we know, is a yellow star. Some stars are white-hot. Sirius is white, and so are Rigel and the two brightest stars in the Southern Cross.

gel is a
ite hot
r which is
thousand
es brighter
n the Sun.

Other stars are cooler than the Sun, and are only red-hot. Betelgeux in Orion is one of these stars. There is another bright red star, called **Antares**, in the constellation of the Scorpion, which from Britain you can see low down in the south during evenings in summer.

17

Sirius is in the constellation of the Great Dog.

You can see Sirius in this photograph.

It is the brightest star in the sky, and has a very faint companion which can only be seen with a powerful telescope.

This photograph shows the double star **Mizar**.

The faint star just above Mizar to the right is Alcor.

One of the stars of Mizar is brighter then the other.

The two stars of Mizar make up a **binary pair**.

BINARY STARS

If you look at the Great Bear, and find the second star in the Bear's tail, you will notice that there is a much fainter star very close beside it. The bright star is **Mizar**. The faint one is called **Alcor**. When the sky is dark and clear, you should be able to find Alcor easily.

If you have a telescope, you will be able to see that Mizar itself is really made up of **two** stars, one rather brighter than the other, and so close together that unless you are using a telescope, they appear as a single star.

18

With some
pairs, the two
stars are
almost equal in
brightness.
These are real
twins.

Path of Binary Stars

In other pairs,
one star is
much brighter
than the other.

If we lived
on a world
moving round
a binary star
the sky would
seem very
strange.

There would be
two suns instead
of one, and they
could be of
different colours.

Albireo in the
constellations
of the Swan is
a binary star
of two colours.
One star is
yellow and the
other blue-
green.

e stars are
le of even
e than two
s.

or in the
stellation
e Twins
ade of six
, four
ht ones and
dim ones.

They make a
beautiful sight.

Double stars of this kind are very common in the sky.
Most of them are real pairs, which have a special
name. We call them **binary stars**. With a binary, the
two stars of the pair move round a point between
them, just as the two bells of a dumb-bell will do if you
turn them round by the wooden bar that joins them.

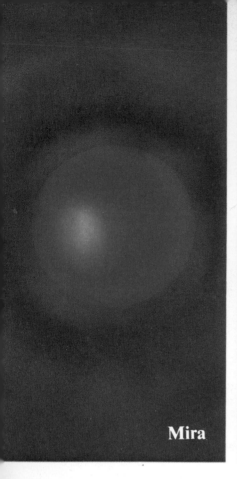

Mira

Mira swollen
and brighter

Mira

Another
variable star
called **Mira**,
name which
means
Wonderful.

It is red, and
when at its
most brilliant
it may become
as bright as the
Pole Star; but
when it is faint
you need a
telescope to see
it.

VARIABLE STARS

Most of the stars shine quite steadily, but there are
some which do not. These are the **variable** stars, which
brighten and fade. They do not seem to wink quickly,
but if you look at them from one night to the next,
you can see that they are changing.

Mira changes
in brightness
because it
swells out and
then shrinks
again.

It reaches its
greatest
brightness
once every
11 months.

Algol

One of these
variable stars is
called **Algol**. It
is made up of
two stars, but
one of them is
much fainter
than the other.

Algol winks
every two
and a half
days.

It gets dimmer
and dimmer for
several hours,
then it stops
fading for about
half an hour
before it begins
to brighten again.

This is
because the
faint star
is passing
in front of
the bright
star. As soon
as the faint
star passes
Algol brightens
up again.

**Path of Algol's
binary stars**

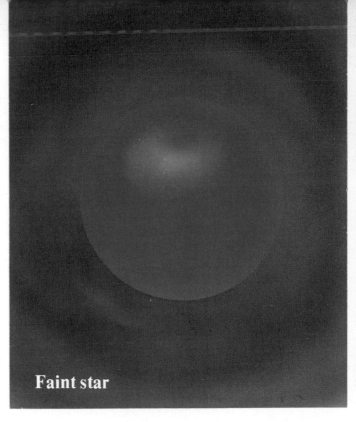

Faint star

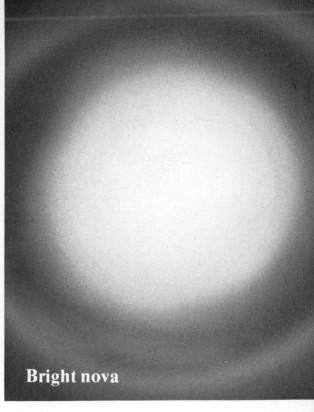

Bright nova

A **nova** is a faint star that brightens up very quickly, and then fades.

The star is exploding, but the explosions are only happening in the outer parts of the star, so the star is not blown to pieces.

You can see this happening in the illustration.

People used to think a nova was caused by two stars colliding together.

Now we know this is not true. The stars are so far apart that they cannot often collide.

There is no danger that our Sun will be hit by another star or turn into a nova.

A NOVA

Now and then, a star which has been very faint will suddenly brighten up quite quickly. In a few days, or even less, it may become thousands of times more brilliant than it has ever been before. A star of this kind is called a **nova**, which comes from a Latin word meaning **new**, even though a nova is not really a new star at all.

Some of these exploding stars have become bright enough to be seen even in daytime, though most of them never become as bright as this.

After the explosion, the star slowly becomes fainter again, until it becomes hard to see even with a big telescope.

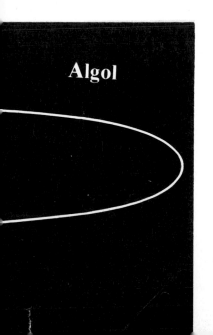

Algol

21

In the above photograph you can see the **Seven Sisters**.

The stars light up clouds of dust and gas around them.

The above photograph shows a **globular** star cluster. It looks like a huge ball of stars.

This cluster is in the constellation of Hercules. It is called Messier 13.

A globular cluster can contain up to a million stars.

If our Sun lay inside a globular cluster we would see many stars brilliant enough to cast shadows, and there would be no darkness at night.

This photograph shows the **Hyades.**

Aldebaran is the bright star on the left. The Hyades make a rough triangle on the right.

Aldebaran is not in the cluster but a long way in front of it, half way between the Hyades and our Earth.

STAR-CLUSTERS

Here and there in the sky you can see **clusters** of stars. The most famous of them is called the **Seven Sisters**. It is very easy to find, not very far from Orion, and it can be seen in the evening sky during winter. Most people can count seven stars in it, but a telescope will show many more. All the brightest stars in the cluster are white, and are much better and more powerful than the Sun.

Another famous star-cluster called the **Hyades** can be seen near the red star, **Aldebaran**, in the constellation of the Bull, between the Seven Sisters and Orion. Many other clusters are known, some of which contain thousands of stars.

NEBULÆ

As we have read, there are many clouds of dust and gas in the sky. We call them **nebulæ**.

The brightest of them can be seen in the constellation of Orion, just below the three bright stars which make up the Hunter's Belt.

The Orion Nebula is easily seen, looking like a tiny patch of shining cloud. Mixed in with it are hot stars, which light up the gas and dust and make it bright.

If a nebula has no stars inside it which are in the right place to make it shine, the gas and dust will stay dark, and will blot out the light of any stars which lie behind it.

In olden times people used to think that dark nebulæ were holes in the sky.

the Southern ross there is very famous ark nebula lled the **Coal ack**.

You can see the Coal Sack in this photograph.

The Coal Sack has no stars inside it to make its dust and gas shine.

It just blots out the stars behind it.

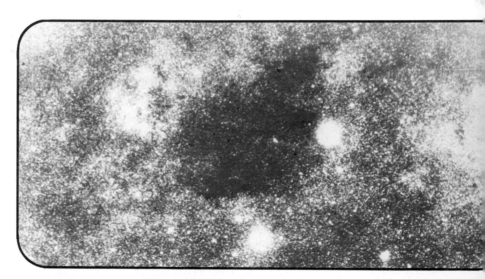

he **Orion ebula** is ery beautiful. has many ot white stars it to make shine.

ou can see his nebula in e opposite hotograph.

This nebula is sometimes called the Sword of Orion, as it marks the place where the Hunter's sword would hang from his belt.

HOW IS A STAR BORN?

How are the stars born, and how do they die?

Stars are of
different ages.
Some are very
young and some
have grown old.

Every star
has a very long
life indeed.

Astronomers of today think that they have gone a
long way toward finding out, even though we do not
know the whole story.

The drawing
show in a
simple way,
different stag
in the
formation of
star.

Cloud of dust
and gas

Cloud shrinks

We cannot
watch a star
throughout
its life, as
the changes
take millions
and millions
of years.

By looking at
different stars
we can work
out how they
are born and
grow old.

A star is born
inside a great
cloud of gas
and dust in
space.

Some of the
gas and dust
begins to
bunch up to
form a star.

The more it
bunches toget
the hotter it
gets inside,
until it begins
to shine.

A star is born inside one of the large clouds of dust
and gas which we can see in space. Because of the
force of gravity, which tries to pull everything inward,
the star shrinks. This makes it grow hotter and hotter
inside, until at last it begins to shine.

24

ur Sun is
hining a
ellow
olour.

a star
hotter
han the
un it will
hine a
lue-white
olour while
is at its
rightest.

A star, such as the Sun, is not burning in the same way as a fire. It is changing one kind of gas into another, and giving off light and heat as it does so. The stars are so big, and have so much gas, that they can go on shining steadily for a very long time, as the Sun is doing now. There are many stars which are much older than either the Sun or the Earth.

The star goes on shining until its gas is used up.

Our Sun has enough gas to last about another 5 thousand million years.

Hot white star

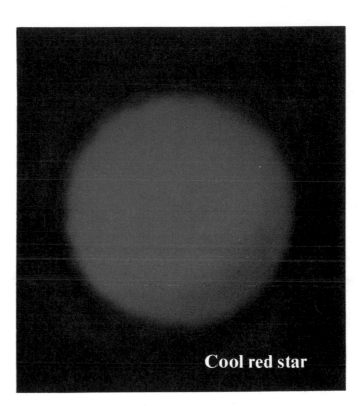

Cool red star

fter its gas is
sed up, the
tar will cool
nd swell out
ntil it is a
uge **red star**.

ig red stars
re known as
ed Giants.

etelgeux is
Red Giant.

HOW DO THE STARS CHANGE?

As the star grows older, it uses up the gas which makes it shine. At last there is so little of this gas left that the star changes completely. Its inside shrinks, and its outside swells out, so that the star becomes bigger but cooler. It turns red and becomes very large. We can see many of these red stars in the sky. Betelgeux, in Orion, and Antares, in the Scorpion, are two of them, and one of the four stars of the Southern Cross is also red.

In about 5 thousand million years time, our Sun will turn into a big red star.

When the Sun changes into a red star, it will be so hot on Earth, that no one will be able to live here.

When the star begins to shrink and becomes small, heavy and white, it is called a **White Dwarf**.

It will go on shining weakly for a long time, but in the end it will become a cold, dark ball.

If you could fill a cup with material from a White Dwarf the cup would weigh more than a large lorry.

When a star blows up, so that most of the star is sent away into space, it is called a **supernova**.

Explosions like this do not happen very often.

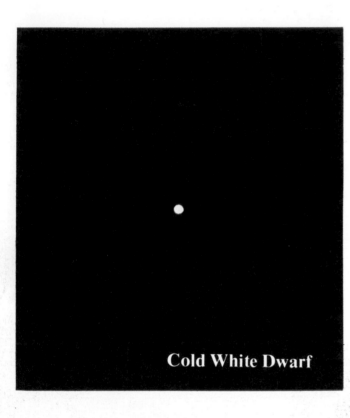

There may be many of these dead stars in the sky, but because they do not give off light, we cannot see them.

Cold White Dwarf

One day the Sun will turn into a small, faint White Dwarf star.

A WHITE DWARF

If the star is the same kind as the Sun, it will then start to shrink again. From being very large and red, it becomes very small and heavy, turning white. A star like that is called a **White Dwarf**.

One famous White Dwarf is the faint companion of Sirius. When the star has used up all its energy, it will become a cold, dead ball.

The Sun will behave in this way, but not for a very long time yet. Indeed, the Sun will not change much for several thousands of millions of years in the future, so that we are in no danger.

A PULSAR

A star which is much bigger and heavier than the Sun may explode, endings its life in a cloud of gas in the middle of which is a very small, faint body which we call a **pulsar**. The best-known of these clouds is the **Crab Nebula.**

Crab ula is all is left of a which was to explode 900 years and h, for a weeks, was ht enough seen even e daytime.

Now it is not bright enough to be seen without a telescope.

All that is left of the old star is a small, heavy object spinning round very quickly. This is called a **pulsar**.

The gas of Crab Nebula is still moving out from the place where the old star exploded.

The Crab Nebula gets its name from the fact that its shape is a little like that of a crab!

You can see the Crab Nebula in the photograph.

THE MILKY WAY

If you are out in the country, well away from street lamps, you will be able to see what looks like a band of light stretching right across the sky. This is called the **Milky Way**. It is made up of stars, though you will need a telescope to see the stars separately.

The stars in the Milky Way seem so close together that they almost touch. This is not really so. Our star-system, which we call the **Galaxy**, is shaped rather like two fried eggs clapped together back-to-back, as shown in the picture.

The Sun, together with the Earth and the rest of its family, lies well away from the centre of the system. When we look along the thickness of the Galaxy, we see many stars in almost the same direction, and it is this which causes the appearance of the Milky Way.

The Milky Way looks like a band of white stretching across the sky.

It is shaped rather like two fried eggs clapped together, back-to-back.

Our Sun is about 32,000 light years from the centre of the Galaxy.

We cannot see all the way through the Galaxy because there is too much gas and dust in the way.

It would take light 100,000 years to cross the Galaxy from one side to the other.

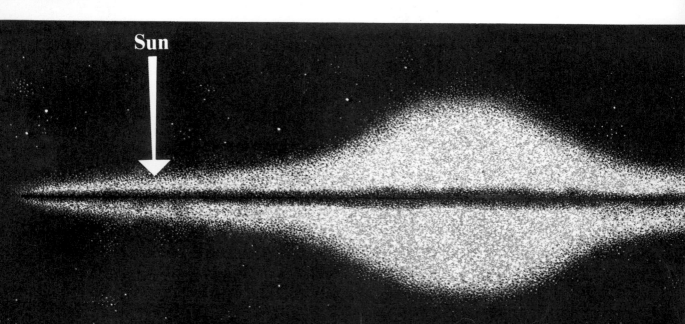

Sun

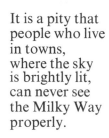

It is a pity that people who live in towns, where the sky is brightly lit, can never see the Milky Way properly.

The Milky Way is a beautiful sight.

There are so many stars in the Milky Way that they look like clouds from a distance.

If we look towards Sagittarius we are looking towards the centre of the Galaxy.

In this photograph of the Scorpion, you can see hundreds of stars from the Milky Way.

· Milky Way

Close together though they look, the stars in the Milky Way are really a very long way away from each other.

There are many hundreds of thousands of stars in our Galaxy.

Our Sun is only one of these stars.

Orbit of Earth round the Sun

Sun's position in the Galaxy

The Sun moves round the centre of the Galaxy.

It takes over 200 million years for the Sun to go round the centre of the Galaxy.

The stars at the centre of the Galaxy travel faster than the Sun.

Our Sun is spinning with the Galaxy at about 250 kilometres (170 miles) per second.

The spiral arms of the Galaxy contain many young white stars.

The stars in the very centre of the Galaxy are mainly old red stars.

There are many galax even larger than our ov

THE GALAXY

The **Galaxy** contains a great many stars, of which our Sun is only one. Between the stars there is dust and gas, and this causes a kind of fog, so that we cannot see right through to the middle of the Galaxy.

Astronomers have found out that the Galaxy is spiral in shape. It is spinning round, and the Sun is moving round the centre of the Galaxy, taking the Earth with it. It takes the Sun over 200 million years to complete one journey.

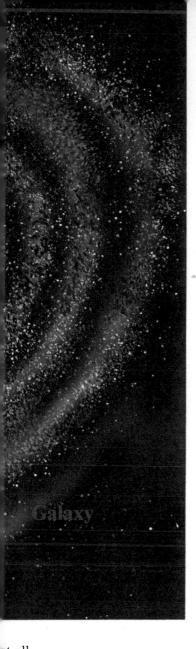

Galaxy

The **Andromeda Galaxy** is larger than our Galaxy. The light that we see from it now first set out before Man lived on Earth, but is is still one of the nearest galaxies to us.

This spiral galaxy is in Pegasus. It is similar in size to our Galaxy, but its arms are more tightly wound.

The galaxy in this photograph is in the constellation of Sculptor.

ot all axies are ral. Some e shaped e balls, have no l outline.

e most tant axies asured so are more n 5000 lion light rs away.

These photographs show some of the galaxies that we can see from Earth.

Their spiral shape is rather like our own Galaxy.

Much further away, well outside our Galaxy, we can see other star-systems of the same kind, some of which are very like our own. Each of these star-systems contains millions of suns, and most people believe that there are other Earths too, even though they are so far away that we cannot see them.

It is very likely that at this moment somebody living on another Earth, going round another sun, is reading a book in just the same way that you have been doing today.

Each of these galaxies is made up of thousands of millions of stars.

INDEX